Pet Sulcata and Leopard Tortoises Care Guide

Sulcata Tortoise (African spurred) and Leopard Tortoise – Buying, Diet, Care, Health (and more…)

By William S Clinton

Foreword

For the past 200 million years, tortoises and turtles have continued their existence relatively unchanged by evolution.

The greatest of the prehistoric turtles, Meiolania, was 8.2 feet (2.5 meters) long, but if this creature were to walk the earth today, it would still be readily recognizable as a tortoise.

The very ubiquitous nature of turtles and tortoises in the animal kingdom gave rise to their symbolic interpretation by a variety of cultures. Typically, the animals have been seen as emblematic of wisdom, strength, and patience.

In America, a number of native tribes believed the earth to be the back of the shell of the celestial Mother Turtle, forever floating on a primordial sea.

From the Maya, who saw turtles as rain gods, to the Chinese who believed a dragon turtle created the earth, these creatures are interwoven in the mythology of diverse peoples scattered around the world.

There seems to be something about the self-contained nature of turtles and tortoises that makes them especially appealing and intriguing to human beings.

Tortoises in particular, with their wise and wizened faces, appear to convey a kind of sturdy self-sufficiency. They

Foreword

seem to be old souls, and look as if they are ready to speak with us about deep matters.

The bigger the tortoise, the greater the fascination it seems to impel, which accounts in part for the growing popularity of Sulcata (African Spurred) and Leopard Tortoises as pets.

These two species are, respectively, the third and fourth largest land tortoises in the world. Both are grazing herbivores from Africa, but with clear differences in their care requirements.

For people who actually know something about Sulcata and Leopard Tortoises, it is not just their size that makes them attractive options as exotic pets. These tortoises are gentle creatures, with a pleasing demeanor.

Unfortunately, unscrupulous dealers often dupe newcomers to the world of tortoises. These unsuspecting people, with every good intention, adopt their tortoises with no real understanding of just how much body mass their new pets will attain in time.

Adult Sulcatas reach a maximum size of 24-36 inches (60-90 cm) and weigh an impressive 100-200 lbs (45.35-90.7 kg).

Adult Leopard Tortoises grow to 18 - 28 inches (45 - 71 cm) and weigh between 40 - 120 lbs (18 - 54 kg).

Additionally, each species can live well past 50 years, with 100 years quite possible for the Sulcata.

Foreword

Once ensconced with a family, the large African tortoises prove themselves to be charming pets, happily coming to their human keepers, and enjoying a nice back rub.

Yes, a tortoise can feel through its shell, and thoroughly enjoys being "petted."

These characteristics of personality make it very difficult for overwhelmed owners to know what to do as their pets get bigger — and bigger — and bigger. Sadly, the result has become a near epidemic of abandoned tortoises.

Zoos won't take former pets. The tortoises cannot survive if released into the wild — and rescue groups are completely overwhelmed.

This information is not presented to discourage you from having a pet tortoise, but to emphasize the absolute necessity that first-time owners know exactly what they're getting into before they adopt either a Sulcata or a Leopard Tortoise.

You must have adequate space to ultimately accommodate the animal's rapid growth, and you must be prepared for a long-term commitment.

There are many factors to consider prior to adoption. In the case of the African Spurred Sulcata, their natural burrowing behavior may prove a problem. As one online blogger put it, Sulcatas can dig holes big enough to bury a Volkswagen!

Foreword

Ultimately, a rural setting is the best environment for an adult Sulcata with space to roam and graze.

Even if the tortoise is small upon acquisition, you will have only about a five-year grace period before your pet reaches 100 pounds / 45.4 kg or more. You may be able to start out with a Sulcata in the backyard, but you'd better have plans to move sooner than later!

Both species are plant eaters, but Leopard Tortoises can eat more of the same vegetables that humans consume. The diet of the Sulcata is more limited.

Obviously, there are pros and cons to owning each species of tortoise. It is vital for the welfare of the tortoise that you understand these things well in advance of adopting one as a pet, which is the purpose of this text.

David Friend, a highly experienced Sulcata tortoise owner, summed up the experience of owning a large tortoise in an article for Tortoise.org, "A Sulcata Here, A Sulcata There, A Sulcata Everywhere." He wrote:

"I am relating my personal experiences with Sulcatas over the last twenty-three years. I have learned and am still learning a lot. Most of my knowledge has come from the animals themselves! As I just stated – observe, observe, observe."

Foreword

Life with a big African Spurred Tortoise will always mean learning new lessons. The intent of this book is to help you determine if the journey is right for you, and to help you take the first few steps along the road if you believe the answer is "yes."

Exclusive FREE Offer

Join other Sulcata and Leopard Tortoise lovers and owners in our unique **FREE** club – Exclusive to owners of this book.

See page 22 on how to join easily in seconds (and free).

Receive discounts on Sulcata and Leopard Tortoise supplies like food and housing. Connect with other members to share knowledge and experience, and ask questions. The best place for lovers of these amazing tortoises.

Table of Contents

Table of Contents

Table of Contents

Table of Contents

Chapter 1 – Meet the Tortoises

The Sulcata Tortoise and the Leopard Tortoise are the third and fourth largest tortoises in the world, falling in line behind the Galapagos (*Geochelone nigra*) and Aldabra (*Geochelone gigantea*) tortoises, respectively.

Other Big Tortoises

The Galapagos Tortoise is a true giant, reaching a maximum length of 5.9 feet (1.8 meters) and a potential weight of more than 800 lbs (363 kg). In addition, this impressive species has been known to live 170 years in captivity.

The Aldabra Tortoise grows to 3.9 feet (1.18 meters) and the largest males will tip the scales at 550 lbs (250 kg).

As a point of comparison, the Leatherback Sea Turtle is the biggest of its kind in the world, attaining a total length of 6.0 to 7.2 feet (1.83-2.2 meters) and weighing 550 to 1,500 lbs (250-680 kg).

Big, Gentle Pets

Sulcata and Leopard Tortoises share relatively common dietary needs, but their natural habitat and behavioral profiles differ significantly.

Chapter 1 – Meet the Tortoises

If you're interested in keeping a large tortoise as a pet, either of these gentle creatures is an excellent choice. This book will help you to decide which tortoise is right for you.

To start, let's become familiar with the basic profiles of both the Sulcata Tortoise (*Geochelone sulcata*) and the Leopard Tortoise (*Stigmochelys pardalis*).

(Note that although both species are native to Africa, their ranges do not overlap.)

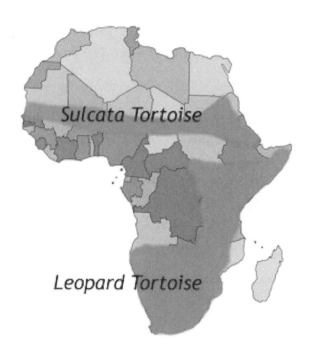

The Sulcata Tortoise

The Sulcata Tortoise is native to the southern edge of the Sahara Desert in northern Africa, in particular a small, 250 mile (402 km) region from Senegal to Eritrea (just north of Ethiopia).

A transitional zone between the Sahara Desert and the Sudan's savannah and forest, the area is covered in grasses, small shrubs, and stunted trees.

Chapter 1 – Meet the Tortoises

It is neither true desert nor savannah, essentially wavering between the two ecosystems depending on the amount of rainfall it receives in any given year.

Sulcata are the third largest tortoise in the world, and the largest of all the mainland tortoises. In the wild, their conservation status is considered "vulnerable" by the International Union for the Conservation of Nature (IUCN).

Physical Characteristics

Adults of the species are 24 - 36 inches (60 – 90 cm) long and weigh an impressive 100-200 lbs (45 -90 kg). They are grazing herbivores with an exceptionally good temperament and a lifespan of 50 to 150 years.

Sulcata are well designed by nature to fit in their quasi-desert home. They have an overall "sandy" coloration with thick yellowish to brown skin and a brown, oval shell or "carapace."

The shell is marked with conspicuous growth rings on each scute or plate that give the species its name. "Sulcus" means furrow or groove. The Sulcata's front legs have large, overlapping scales, while the hind legs sport conical spurs.

The Sulcata is often confused with the Spur-Thighed Tortoise (*Testudo graeca*). Another handsome creature, the Spur-Thighed Tortoise is also an herbivore native to a semi-arid climate (the Mediterranean), but reaches a maximum size of just 7.8 inches (19.8 cm).

Chapter 1 – Meet the Tortoises

To avoid confusion, you will often see *Testudo graeca* referred to as the Greek Tortoise. There is still, however, considerable confusion between the two species.

Burrowing Animals

During the monsoon season in their native range, Sulcatas dig burrows they will use to shelter themselves from the blistering temperatures of the dry season. Year round, these same refuges will protect the creatures from the mid-day sun.

(It is a misconception that these tortoises can take hours in the direct sun when kept as pets. They must have shelter and shade, or they can easily succumb to heat stroke and die.)

A Sulcata's burrow may be as deep as 20 feet (6.1 meters) and cover a horizontal distance of more than 30 feet (9.1 meters). These tortoises are regular engineers, designing multiple "rooms" and connecting the entire layout with a system of tunnels.

By developing this subterranean environment for itself, the Sulcata creates a more stable environment than that found on the surface. Sulcata burrows have a more constant temperature and higher levels of humidity, often more than 50 percent.

During the dry season, Sulcata rarely leave their underground homes. As the rainy season approaches, the tortoise comes to the surface to look for food and to find water.

This emergence from the burrow also coincides with the most likely time for mating, but there is no specific breeding season for these tortoises in the wild.

Breeding in the Wild

Breeding occurs year round for the simple fact that there are not huge populations of Sulcatas. When males and females meet up, they simply take advantage of the opportunity.

In the wild, females will typically deposit their eggs at the bases of bushes, leaving as many as 24 eggs that will hatch in 100-200 days. In captivity, the female Sulcata will look for the base of some structure to dig her nest.

Feeding Patterns

Feeding patterns follow the same opportunistic path. When the rains are falling, the tortoises can enjoy a diet of grasses and weeds along with leaves and fruits.

As the months pass and things dry out, however, they eat whatever they can find. This includes such items as bark and small branches, the feces of other animals, and even carrion if no other food source is available.

Distinguishing Gender

It is impossible to tell male and female Sulcata apart until the individual specimen has reached a weight of at least 10-15 lbs / 4.5-6.8 kg.

At that size, males develop a concave plastron, which is the ventral or underside of the shell.

The male's anal scutes also form a "V" at the point at which the tail protrudes from the body, and the tail itself is much longer than that found in females.

Females have a more elongated overall shape, with a flat plastron, and the anal scutes form a "U" shape. The larger the tortoise grows, the more pronounced each of these characteristics will become.

Sulcata Summary:

- Third largest land tortoise in the world
- Maximum size 2'-3' (0.6-0.9 meters)
- Maximum weight 100-200 lbs. (45.35-90.7 kg)
- Lifespan 50-150 years
- Grazing herbivore
- Sandy coloration with brown skin
- Conical spurs on the hind legs
- Burrowing tortoises

- Average clutch size 24 eggs
- Incubation period 100-200 days
- Males greater than 10-15 lbs. / 4.5-6.8 kg have a concave plastron and anal scutes that form a "V"
- Females have a flat plastron, an elongated oval shape, and anal scutes that form a "U"

The Leopard Tortoise

The Leopard Tortoise is native to the savannahs of eastern and southern Africa from the Sudan to the Cape. It is a grazing species of the semi-arid grasslands and is the fourth largest of the land tortoises.

At the northern end of its range, the Leopard Tortoise is most active in the aftermath of the rainy season, with decreasing activity in drier months after the fashion of the Sulcata Tortoise.

In the central and southern regions, the Leopard Tortoise actually goes into a sort of hibernation, seeking shelter from cooler weather in abandoned animal burrows or any similar sanctuary it can find.

Although shy and fond of hiding, the Leopard Tortoise does not dig its own burrows.

Physical Characteristics

Adults reach a maximum size of 18-28 inches (45.72-71.12 cm) and weigh between 40-120 lbs (18.14-54.43 kg). They have a lifespan of 80 to 100 years.

The carapace of these species is domed and high, making the tortoise appear to be "tall." Overall, the body conformation is more round than long.

It is quite common for the scutes or scales in this species to take on a pyramid-like shape. This formation is seen in roughly 50% of individuals including wild specimens. In other varieties of tortoise, however, it occurs only in captivity.

Additionally, the Leopard Tortoise's shell is marked with black spots, blotches, stripes and dashes in a unique and recognizable pattern per individual.

This "leopard"-like patterning is the origin of the tortoise's common name, and one of the most visually attractive things about this species.

The background color of the carapace and of the tortoise's skin is cream colored to yellow. The contrast between the skin and the intricately marked shell is both striking and handsome.

Feeding Habits and Breeding

Like the Sulcata Tortoise, the Leopard Tortoise feeds on grass, weeds, and various leaves. They, too, will eat the feces of other animals, and will resort to carrion if need be.

In captivity, the Leopard Tortoise is somewhat easier to feed as it can eat more of the same kind of produce humans consume.

The Leopard Tortoise breeds from the springtime into the late fall. A female can lay three or more clutches of 5-20 eggs, which can take from 90-400 days to hatch.

Distinguishing Gender

Differentiating between male and female leopard tortoises can be difficult when they are young. As the tortoise grows, there are several key differences that you can observe. When fully grown, the female leopard tortoise tends to be larger than the male. However it should be noted that the male leopard tortoise can sometimes be larger. The female leopard tortoise generally has a higher dome and a more rounded shape.

Another key difference is that the male leopard tortoise has a longer and thicker tail. Additionally, the male leopard tortoise has a "v" shaped notch around the tail and the female has a "u" shaped notch around the tail. The male plastron will be concave and in comparison the female plastron will be flat. Although it can sometimes appear to be difficult to distinguish between the genders, the differences are very pronounced when the tortoises are observed side by side.

Leopard Tortoise Summary:

- Fourth largest land tortoise in the world
- Maximum size 18-28 inches (45.72-71.12 cm)
- Maximum weight 40-120 lbs (18.14-54.43 kg)
- Lifespan 80 to 100 years
- Grazing herbivore
- Cream to yellow coloration with distinctive black marks on the shell
- Shy and likes to hide, but does not burrow
- Average clutch size 5-20 eggs
- Incubation period 90-400 days

Chapter 1 – Meet the Tortoises

Exclusive FREE Offer – How to Join

Join other Sulcata and Leopard tortoise lovers in our unique **FREE** club – Exclusive to owners of this book (and receive **free updates** to this book in the future)

It's quick and easy to sign up. You can receive discounts on tortoise food, supplies and more including connecting with other owners. Here's how in 2 simple steps…

Step 1

Go to http://www.TortoiseBook.com

Enter your name and email address and click "Join"

Step 2

Confirm your subscription. As soon as you sign up we'll send you an email asking you to confirm the details are correct. Just click the link in the email and you'll be joined free.

If you don't receive the email, please check your spam folder and that you used the correct email address.

It's as easy as that. Any questions please email support@tortoisebook.com and where possible we will help.

Chapter 2 – Buying a Tortoise

Sulcata and Leopard Tortoises are commonly purchased as pets, but sadly, many initially enthusiastic owners just do not realize how big these creatures get.

Since zoos will not take in cast off pets, many tortoises are dumped in the wild because there are so few rescue groups to save them.

Neither species is well suited to life outside their native climates without adequate husbandry from keepers, so it's common for abandoned specimens to freeze to death, or to succumb to heat and dehydration.

What to Know Before You Buy

It is imperative that you understand exactly what you are doing before you adopt a Sulcata or Leopard Tortoise.

In tortoise terms, you're essentially adopting grazing "livestock." You don't quite need a barn to keep one of these creatures, but it's not going to live in some cute little aquarium, either.

Get Big Fast!

Tortoises are more active than you think. They gain weight and size fast. With good conditions, you can expect your Sulcata to reach 100 pounds (45.4 kg) in 5 years or less, with the Leopard Tortoise not far behind in terms of development.

If you are planning on keeping the tortoise inside, size will ultimately present a problem. Most people start out with a habitat known as a tortoise "table," but expect your pet to outgrow that arrangement quickly.

Be Cautious with Other Pets

If you are keeping a tortoise inside, you must keep it safe from other pets. When kept outside, the tortoise needs protection from wild animals. Never assume that either a dog or a cat will simply ignore a tortoise.

Chapter 2 – Buying a Tortoise

A dog could regard a tortoise as a chew toy and wound the creature badly. When they get large enough, a tortoise can try to defend itself and the wounds will go in the other direction.

Bottom line: Don't leave other pets and tortoises together unsupervised. Interactions are entirely dependent on individual personalities and there is no way to guess how it will go.

Tortoises and Children

If children are to be involved in the care of the tortoise or will be interacting with it, they need to be supervised and properly instructed.

This is especially crucial when the tortoises are young. If their shells have not hardened, and they are dropped or stepped on, the creature can suffer fatal internal damage, or be crippled for life.

Really young children may even think it's safe to throw a tortoise, reasoning that the apparently rigid shell will serve as ample protection.

This is far from the case. A tortoise's shell is not "armor," and these creatures can be severely injured if not handled properly.

Do not let children care for tortoises without the guidance and input of a responsible and knowledgeable adult.

Multiple Tortoises

If you decide you want to keep more than one tortoise, you not only need adequate space, but be prepared to be a referee.

Male Sulcata tortoises will fight, and they can inflict more damage on one another than you may realize.

(Hormonal aggression is less prevalent in Leopard Tortoise males and they can generally be housed in groups without incident.)

When Sulcata males fight, the most typical wounds that result are to the head, neck, and eyes. Dominant males will tip smaller tortoises over on their backs.

This is very dangerous. If the smaller tortoise cannot right itself, it may suffer from fatal heat stroke.

Only consider keeping multiple tortoises if you have sufficient acreage for the creatures to work out issues of territoriality.

Make sure you have access to an exotic animal veterinarian to treat any open wounds. Tortoises have a tendency to develop abscesses, so cuts, abrasions, and bites must be tended to promptly.

Chapter 2 – Buying a Tortoise

Protection Against the Weather

Tortoises are poikilotherms. They rely on the surrounding conditions for the regulation of their body temperature and correct metabolic function.

Both the Sulcata and the Leopard Tortoise need to be able to seek shade during the hottest part of the day, and they require a good source of water and some humidity.

It is a huge mistake to assume that just because these tortoises are from Africa, they can take any degree of heat. They are just as susceptible to extreme cold. Tortoises housed outside will need a shelter or "barn" as protection from the elements.

Optimal temperatures for both species fall in the range of 75-85 °F (23-29 °C).

Tortoises Need Space!

Remember that you are adopting a grazing herbivore. Estimates vary, but for truly large specimens of either species, you're looking at half an acre to a full acre to keep them happy.

This is a matter of heated discussion in online tortoise discussion forums, with some people pointing out, quite correctly, that without room to roam according to their nature, tortoises get bored.

They will thrive in an outdoor enclosure, but if you live in the city, you'll essentially be giving up your backyard and rearranging the landscape frequently to keep your tortoise interested.

And don't think you're going to be raising lush grass with a Sulcata or Leopard Tortoise around! They'll decimate your landscape in short order.

Neither species is recommended for apartment dwellers unless you adopt the tortoises when they are very small and have plans to move into accommodations with a yard, or situated on land in the country.

Options for Buying a Tortoise

It is not difficult to locate a Sulcata or Leopard Tortoise for sale, the following venues are the most viable options.

(Note, however, that I have devoted several pages to discussing tortoise rescue groups and that this is the method of acquisition I most strongly support.)

Pet Shops

Due to the increasing popularity of Sulcata and Leopard Tortoises, it is possible to purchase them in some pet shops, particularly specialty reptile shops. There are both advantages and disadvantages to going this route.

Chapter 2 – Buying a Tortoise

If a shop sells tortoises, they are more likely to keep merchandise in stock to help you care for your pet.

This does not mean, however, that you can turn to the shop for advice as your tortoise grows — unless you are lucky enough to find a store that specializes in nothing but reptiles.

While it is not impossible to find such a store, it is difficult unless you are in a major metropolitan area. If you live within reasonable driving distance, however, it may be worth it to avail yourself of expert advice.

In an ideal situation, however, you will be able to locate a breeder who not only raises tortoises, but who also lives with them. This will allow you to have someone to whom you can turn with problems and concerns.

Breed Clubs and Reptile Shows

Since the 1990s, reptile breed clubs have become increasingly popular. Many have an online presence, and are tied to reptile shows held regionally throughout the year.

These shows not only allow enthusiasts to meet and discuss their hobbies, but they can often be venues for breeders to offer animals for sale or to connect with potential clients for future sales.

Chapter 2 – Buying a Tortoise

(See the end matter at the back of this book for a list of relevant websites to find discussion forums and other sites to help you connect with other African tortoise enthusiasts and breeders.)

A Word About Buying Online

The end matter also includes online sources to purchase both species of African tortoises. There is some truth to the assertion that almost anything, including live animals can be purchased online.

Just because it is possible to do so, however, does not mean it is a good idea.

I am not a fan of shipping live animals. Young African tortoises are sensitive creatures, subject to severe physical stress when confronted with changes in temperature and hydration.

Young tortoises have shells that have not yet hardened. These small creatures can be crushed easily, suffering potentially fatal internal injuries.

If they survive such an accident, the hatchling may be crippled for life, suffering years of hardship due to human negligence.

Typically only these small and vulnerable hatchlings are offered for sale online because they can be shipped more easily, and, frankly, because they are "cuter."

Do not think that "live delivery" guarantees mean any special care is being taken. This is a reference to speed of delivery only.

Shipping live animals is, in my opinion, an inhumane practice and one that should not be encouraged or supported.

We strongly recommend purchasing a tortoise in person and transporting the animal safely to your home yourself.

This is absolutely essential in buying a larger specimen because the shipping costs for a big tortoise can be prohibitive.

Chapter 2 – Buying a Tortoise

Estimated Buying Costs

Although prices will vary widely, you can expect to see hatchlings for both species offered in the range of $90-$150 / £56.20-£93.70.

Adults can be priced anywhere up to $1000 / £625 each.

Tortoise Rescue Groups

In the special section following this chapter, we will discuss tortoise rescue groups in full and provide contact information.

Both Sulcata and Leopard Tortoises are left homeless in large numbers each year. This is a serious problem for both species.

There are many tortoises in need of new homes, and this is the method of adoption I most strenuously encourage.

The harsh reality is that homeless African tortoises die every year because they are released into the wild and are unable to survive without human intervention.

If you can get in touch with one of these rescue groups and take in an orphaned tortoise, this is an outstanding way to both acquire a pet and to connect with people who will help you understand exactly how to care for the animal's particular needs.

If you adopt from a rescue group ALWAYS make a donation to support the continued work of the organization.

Signs of a Healthy Tortoise

In evaluating the health of any tortoise you are considering adopting, look for the following signs:

Chapter 2 – Buying a Tortoise

- Healthy tortoises are alert and active. Don't believe the stereotype that tortoises are slow and just sit around doing nothing. These guys can move!

- Leopard Tortoises are shyer than Sulcatas, but they should still be obviously alert and interested.

- Make sure the tortoise is eating and drinking.

- The overall look of the body should be strong. A dehydrated tortoise will have sunken eyes and its skin will be excessively loose and hanging in folds around the head and limbs.

- The eyes should be fully open and expressive. Many tortoise owners swear they see a "twinkle" in their pet's eyes.

- Make sure the nostrils are dry and clear. A runny or wet nose can be a sign of illness.

Inactive tortoises that just sit there, or worse yet don't come out of their shells are not in good shape!

Special Section: Tortoise Rescue

There is a tremendous and on-going need for abandoned Sulcata and Leopard Tortoises to be placed in new homes. These creatures became popular in the 1990s, about the same time that people were buying iguanas.

Why is There a Need for Rescues?

Both classes of pet owners suffered from the same problem. Pet stores did not provide accurate information for just how big these creatures really become.

The iguana owners, in time, wound up with a six-foot long / 1. 8 meter aggressive lizard. The tortoise owners found themselves trying to husband a 100+ lb / 45+ kg mini "tank."

Since the tortoises, however, are hardy and personable, it is still possible to see hundreds of hatchlings for sale at reptile shows across the nation.

(Bear in mind that in the United States, it is illegal to sell any turtle or tortoise of less than 4 in/10.16 cm in length.)

The biggest lie prospective tortoise owners are told? "It won't get larger than its tank." Wrong!

Know What You're Getting Into!

Don't even think you can keep a Sulcata or Leopard tortoise in an aquarium. These animals grow fast and they grow BIG. Ultimately, they grow too big to even be kept indoors at all.

Sulcatas, in particular, are burrowing animals. They dig vociferously, and can easily shove furniture around. Since they don't hibernate, when they're kept outdoors during the winter, they require a heated enclosure.

Abandoned Tortoises

For many owners who acquired their tortoises on impulse and without research, the realities of African tortoise husbandry proved to be too much.

A large percentage of these people approached zoos only to be turned away. Zoos won't take former pets, and there's virtually no market for adult tortoises, making resale next to impossible.

Over-crowded tortoise and reptile rescue groups run out of space fast. It's incredibly difficult to find someone to take an animal that needs half an acre or more to roam, plus male tortoises tend to fight when housed together.

In the truly tragic cases, the tortoises are released into the wild where they either starve or freeze to death.

During the time that they do survive, they may well infect native wildlife with parasites or diseases. Wild release is never a good idea -- for any kind of exotic species.

Consider a Re-Homed Tortoise

If you have the space and are genuinely interested in having a Sulcata or Leopard Tortoise, I strongly urge you to consider adopting one of these abandoned pets.

The rescue groups listed below, and others like them, are strained to the breaking point, but still doing incredible work to save these magnificent creatures.

These organizations need people to take in abandoned tortoises and to give them the time, attention, and care they deserve.

Special Section: Tortoise Rescue

Even if you have decided that a Sulcata or Leopard Tortoise is too much for you to care for on your own, all such groups need both funds and volunteers.

It's completely possible for you to have these tortoises in your life without taking one on as a pet. If you're still undecided about adopting, volunteer work with a rescue group may help you to make a decision.

The plight of abandoned African tortoises has not been widely publicized because these are such highly specialized animals that suffer from long-held stereotypes.

Surely a tortoise is the world's most boring pet? Wrong again. Sulcata and Leopard Tortoises have wonderful personalities. They are highly interactive, extremely intelligent, and bond with their human keepers.

These creatures did not ask to be misrepresented by unscrupulous breeders and owners of pet stores intent on cashing in on their popularity.

The tortoises themselves are just trying to go about their lives being tortoises. They need what they need, and cannot simply change to accommodate us.

You can help these abandoned animals by supporting the efforts of tortoise rescue groups in any way that fits both your lifestyle and your budget.

Special Section: Tortoise Rescue

This is very much a case of lovely exotic animals in need of the caring help of compassionate human beings.

Given the fact that both species of African tortoises can live well in excess of 50 years, there is no "short changing" yourself in adopting a rescue tortoise -- quite to the contrary.

You will not only be acquiring a gentle and loving companion animal that will be with you for many years to come, but you will also likely be saving a life.

Special Section: Tortoise Rescue

An Added Advantage

As an added advantage to adopting through a rescue group, you will automatically make contact with people knowledgeable in keeping Sulcata and Leopard Tortoises.

It will be to your benefit to be able to get advice about creating the right environment for your new pet, and meeting all of its needs, from diet to shelter.

Being part of the larger community of African tortoise owners can help to ensure that both you and your pet have the best chance to spend many happy years together.

Special Section: Tortoise Rescue

American Tortoise Rescue
http://www.tortoise.com

CA Turtle and Tortoise Club Rescue and Adoption Programs
http://www.tortoise.org/cttc/adoption.html

San Diego Turtle and Tortoise Society
http://www.sdturtle.org

Gulf Coast Turtle and Tortoise Society
http://www.gctts.org/rescue

Tortoise Protection Group
http://www.tortoise-protection-group.org.uk/site/131.asp

Turtle Rescue USA
http://www.turtlerescueusa.com/wordpress/?page_id=4

The Clovis Turtle & Tortoise Rescue
http://www.clovisturtlerescue.tripod.com

Rio Grande Turtle and Tortoise Club
http://www.rgttc.org

Mid-Atlantic Turtle & Tortoise Society
http://www.matts-turtles.org/adoptions.html

Special Section: Tortoise Rescue

Virginia Reptile Rescue, Inc.
http://www.vareptilerescue.org

Turtopia – Rescue, Rehabilitation, Rehoming
http://www.turtopia.tripod.com

Herp Societies and Rescues
http://www.anapsid.org/societies/

Arrowhead Reptile Rescue
http://www.arrowheadreptilerescue.org/

Turtle Rescue of Long Island
http://www.turtlerescues.org/sulcata_tortoise.htm

Ojai Sulcata Project
http://www.ojaisulcataproject.org/

Western Mass Turtle Rescue
http://www.westernmassturtlerescue.org/

My New Turtle
http://www.mynewturtle.com/

Rescue Groups in the UK

Tortoise Protection Group
http://www.tortoise-protection-group.org.uk/site/124.asp

East Midlands Open Rescue
openrescue.weebly.com/tortoises.html

Tortoise Trust
http://www.tortoisetrust.org/

British Chelonia Group
http://www.britishcheloniagroup.org.uk

Beaver Water World
http://www.beaverwaterworld.com

Chapter 3 – Daily Tortoise Care

In order to provide husbandry recommendations for each species, the sub-headings later in this chapter will be divided accordingly between "Sulcata" and "Leopard."

When you see a heading that is not preceded by a species name, the information in that section can be applied to both.

Selecting a Habitat

The kind of habitat you will use for your tortoise will depend entirely on its age and size. For hatchlings of up to five years that weigh less than 15 lbs / 6.8 kg, you can use an indoor "tortoise table."

This will not, however, negate the need to create an outdoor area with a good mix of sun and shade where your pet will spend time every day.

Tortoises not only need to be outside to get adequate exercise, they need sunshine to absorb Vitamin D3 in their systems.

Designing a Tortoise Table

For a tortoise table to adequately address the needs of your pet, it will likely take up as much as 25 sq ft / 2.32 sq m of the room in which it is placed.

(As a point of comparison, a regulation table tennis or "ping pong" table is 45 sq ft / 4.18 sq m.)

Protective Surface

If housing Sulcatas, the surface area of the table should be covered in ceramic tile or a similar durable material to prevent the creatures from following their natural instinct to burrow.

This will also help to protect the surface of the table from any water splashed out of the tortoise's "bowl" and facilitate cleaning.

Border the surface area of the table with "walls" that are at least 10 in / 25.4 cm high. If the tortoises can see out, they will often try to climb the walls, fall, and injure themselves.

Water "Dish"

Rather than a conventional water bowl, use a saucer-like dish to create a "pool" for your tortoise. The saucer should be commensurate with the size of your pet.

The tortoise should be able to walk completely into the "pool" and get out easily. Obviously, given this behavior, you will need to change the water frequently to keep it clean.

Since tortoises like to shove things around and rearrange them, you may want to wedge the water saucer in place with heavy bricks or rocks.

You can see some water dishes at
TortoiseBook.com/dish.htm (USA)
TortoiseBook.com/dishuk.htm (UK)

Substrate

Cover the table with an appropriate substrate. A mixture of organic material like sphagnum moss, or a product like Bed-A-Beast or Eco Earth Brick with grass hay is a good option.

Dampen the substrate once or twice a week to keep a good level of humidity.

Expect to need about 15 gallons / 57 liters of substrate to cover the entire table.

Bed-A-Beast and Eco Earth Brick sell for approximately $3 / £2. Each product is made of coconut fiber.

You can see some Tortoise Substrate at
TortoiseBook.com/bedding.htm (US)
TortoiseBook.com/beddinguk.htm (htm)

Light for Basking

When kept inside, your tortoise will need to be provided with a basking area. This can be achieved with a mixture of full-spectrum UV bulbs and incandescent heat lamps or bulbs that provide both benefits.

Zoo Med sells self-ballasted 100-watt Powersun UVB heat bulbs for approximately $45-$50 / £28-£31 each.

You will need to monitor the temperature of the table to keep it in the optimum range of 75-85 °F (23-29 °C). The basking area, however, should be much warmer.

Sulcata Tortoises prefer to bask in spots that reach temperatures of 95-100 °F / 35-38 °C, while Leopard Tortoises are happy with 95 °F / 35 °C.

Tortoise Lamps
TortoiseBook.com/lamps.htm (USA)
TortoiseBook.com/lampsuk.htm (UK)

Provide a Burrow

Sulcatas are burrowing animals, and Leopard Tortoises like to hide in areas they locate, so provide some kind of hiding spot for your pet.

You can accomplish this by covering a portion of the table with solid boards, and then hanging canvas "curtains" off the leading edge down to the substrate.

This arrangement will make the burrow dark and comfortable for the tortoise, but allow you to pull the curtains back for cleaning and maintenance.

Designing a Tortoise Shed

When your tortoise is too large to remain in the house, and too big for you to carry, your pet will need to be moved outdoors.

The outdoor enclosure must include a shed or barn to protect the tortoise at night and during bad weather.

This structure can be something you build on your own, hire a contractor to build, or buy ready-made as in a dog house or small, pre-fabricated gardening shed.

It is important, however, that the structure be both insulated and heated. Failure to do so can have tragic consequences.

Most of North America and the UK are too cold for either species of African tortoise to stay outdoors year round. Heat mats are the preferred option for winter warming for these tortoises.

The Osborne Standfield Heat Pad is an excellent choice, and is widely used in zoos. The watertight pads are designed for even heat distribution with the heating element sealed in rigid fiberglass.

Prices vary by size, but a 3' x 3' / .9 x .9 meter square heating pad retails for $185 / £115.

Depending on your circumstances, the tortoise's yard (which may be your yard as well) should be fenced to protect your pet from other animals.

It is advisable to have a smaller yard to which your tortoise can be confined at night for its safety.

Sulcata - Managing Diet

There are some common mistakes new Sulcata owners make in feeding their pets. At the top of the list is a failure to provide enough fiber, followed closely by feeding too much protein.

Sulcatas do not get a lot of protein in their diet naturally. Abnormally large amounts will stress their liver and kidneys. If this imbalance is accompanied by poor hydration, the tortoise's shell will begin to show pyramiding.

Do not try to give your tortoise the kind of produce you would eat. Even dark leafy greens have too much protein for the Sulcata to thrive.

Fruits and any sugary foods are equally bad because they disrupt the pH levels (acidity) of the digestive tract causing the beneficial bacteria in the gut to die off. This allows toxins to permeate the bowel tract and to enter the bloodstream.

It is also necessary to provide your pet with calcium, and to watch the calcium-phosphorous balance in the diet.

Dietary items that hinder calcium absorption include broccoli and mustard greens among other members of the brassicae family. These include, but are not limited to:

- Kale
- Collard greens
- Cabbage
- Brussels sprouts
- Cauliflower
- Bok choy
- Rutabaga
- Arugula
- Radish

Do not overfeed! Reptiles have slow metabolisms. They don't need as much food as you think — or that they think, for that matter. Like any pet, a Sulcata is perfectly capable of begging for treats. Don't fall for it!

Sulcata - Dietary Basics

The staples of your Sulcata's diet should be fresh and dried grasses including:

- Bermuda grass
- Orchard grass
- Big Bluestem

- Little Bluestem
- Western Wheatgrass
- Blue Grama
- Arizona Fescue
- Lawn Fescue
- Sheep Fescue
- Creeping Red Fescue

Do not feed more than 10 percent of the total diet in alfalfa or clover.

You can also feed your tortoise a variety of edible flowers, leaves, and weeds including:

- Dandelion
- The pads of prickly pear cactus (spines removed)
- Broadleaf or Buckhorn Plantains
- Globe Mallow
- Henbit
- Hollyhock
- Roses (flowers only)
- Sowthistle
- Chickweed
- Hibiscus
- Geranium
- Mulberry leaves
- Grape leaves

DO NOT feed your tortoise:

- Dog or cat food
- Dairy or cheese products
- Any kind of legumes (beans or peas)
- Any soy-based product
- Grains like corn, wheat, barley, or rye

Commercial tortoise diets really are not recommended for Sulcatas. These are grazing animals and they will do best when they are fed accordingly.

Many owners simply go to their local feed store and buy the same kind of pasture mix hay that would be used with horses.

You can grow your own grasses for your tortoise, but you may not be able to stay ahead of your Sulcata. They can decimate a plot of land much more quickly than you might think.

Sulcata - Calcium Needs

If you live in a region that is classed as semi-arid to arid, the calcium levels in the soil should be high. So long as you feed your tortoise locally grown hay, you should not have to provide a calcium supplement for your pet.

If, however, your area is humid and rainy, the soil will contain little calcium and you will need to give your tortoise a supplement.

Choose a supplement that does NOT include phosphorous, which your pet should already be deriving from a well-balanced diet.

The easiest way to provide your Sulcata with calcium is to buy a large cuttlebone for the tortoise. Try to find one that is at least 10 inches (25.4 cm) in length.

(There will be a shell-like hard backing on the cuttlebone that should be removed.)

Expect to pay approximately $3 / £1.87 for a cuttlebone of that size. If you find a good price or a ready supplier, stock up. Sulcatas enjoy chewing on cuttlebones and will crunch through them steadily.
Break the cuttlebone into pieces and scatter them around your pet's enclosure. If you prefer to use a powdered supplement, buy a human formulation with either calcium citrate or calcium maleate.

Once a week grind a tablet or open a capsule, mix it with a can of pumpkin pie filler, and give it to the tortoise. Your pet will regard this as a fine treat and won't realize there's a dose of "medicine" involved.

(For a 200 count bottle of calcium tablets, 600 mg each, you will pay approximately $12 / £7.5.)

Chapter 3 – Daily Tortoise Care

Sulcata - Water and Humidity

Your Sulcata should always have clean, fresh water available. As challenging as it may sound, you're going to have to find a water saucer big enough for your tortoise to climb into if it's of a mind to go wading.

Using a "pool" rather a bowl for your tortoise accomplishes two things. It not only gives your pet a source of clean drinking water, but it allows the tortoise to derive additional hydration from soaking.

The saucer has to be shallow, however, or your pet could drown. As your tortoise gets larger, you will likely find yourself using some variation of a child's wading pool, or creating some other shallow pond structure.

(You may have to get creative, so it's difficult to guess at the cost of this necessary requirement.)

Use a deep layer of sphagnum moss, Bed-A-Beast, or Eco Earth Brick in one corner of your pet's enclosure to create a damp sleeping place, which will also help to fight off dehydration.

(Again, these substrate products sell for approximately $3 / £2. Remember to moisten the material before you place it in your tortoise's habitat.)

It's recommended that you give your tortoise a good soak once a week for about 15 minutes in shallow water. When you can no longer pick up your pet, you may have to tempt it into the pool with a treat.

In the wild, Sulcatas burrow deep into the earth creating densely humid microclimates for themselves. In captivity, they need our help to have access to the level of moisture they require.

Hatchlings up to the age of one year will need to be soaked daily. From age 1-5, soak two to three times per week. Use warm water, at a level only deep enough to reach your pet's neck. The container should be thoroughly rinsed and dried after each soak.

Tortoise Products

Amazon have a great range of tortoise products from bedding, food, water dishes and lots more. You can see everything on one page by visiting

TortoiseBook.com/products.htm (USA)
TortoiseBook.com/productsuk.htm (UK)

Leopard - Notes on Housing

Although the general comments made on housing in the beginning of this chapter can be adapted to either tortoise,

there are some special considerations regarding the somewhat smaller Leopard Tortoise.

Remember that this species reaches a maximum size of 18-28 inches (45.72-71.12 cm) and weighs between 40-120 lbs. At a minimum, they require an enclosure of 10 ft x 10 ft / 3m x 3m for no more than two tortoises.

For this species, make opaque bounding walls that are at least 18 in / 46 cm high. The good news is that Leopard Tortoises are not known to be adept at staging great escapes. They don't burrow, and they aren't aggressive.

This is a huge difference from the Sulcata Tortoise. You can quite easily keep multiple Leopard Tortoises together. Male Leopards will not display aggression and fight.

Their outdoor enclosures should include:

- A hide box
- Shrubs and/or grasses (also for hiding)
- A patch of bare dirt for rolling
- A slope for basking

The Leopard Tortoise is shyer than the Sulcata, so it's very important to give these creatures enough places to tuck themselves away from sight that they feel secure.

When housed indoors, make sure their basking spot reaches a temperature of 95 °F / 35 °C and is balanced against a cool side of the habitat that is at least 10 degrees cooler.

Also be sure the Leopard Tortoise has a full-spectrum UVB light which is essential for Vitamin D3 to allow for calcium absorption.

If housed outdoors, use a heating mat for this species as described at the beginning of this chapter.

Leopard - Managing Diet

Leopard Tortoises require a calcium-rich diet that is high in fiber in keeping with their natural grazing habits. In the wild, they live on a variety of grasses and other vegetation.

The same kinds of hays should be used with this species as with Sulcatas, namely:

- Bermuda grass
- Orchard grass
- Big bluestem
- Little bluestem
- Western wheatgrass
- Blue grama
- Arizona fescue
- Lawn fescue
- Sheep fescue
- Creeping red fescue

About twice a week, supplement this vegetation with:

- Cactus pads with the spines removed
- Grape leaves
- Mustard greens
- Dandelion greens and flowers
- Escarole
- Collard greens
- Mulberry leaves

- Pumpkin
- Zucchini
- Butternut squash
- Turnip greens
- Yellow squash
- Hibiscus leaves and flowers
- Mushrooms
- Sweet potatoes
- Carrots
- Bell peppers

A very small portion of the diet, no more than 5%, can be drawn from the following:

- Apples
- Tomatoes
- Cantaloupe
- Papayas
- Watermelon
- Strawberries
- Honeydew
- Raspberries
- Mangos
- Grapes
- Bananas

If your Leopard Tortoise is provided with a varied diet, and is given access to UVB light there should be no need for supplementation.

Hatchlings, however, should have their food lightly sprinkled with calcium powder several days a week.

If there is a concern about proper vitamin and mineral levels, provide your Leopard Tortoise with a cuttlebone, and purchase Vitamin D3 powder to sprinkle on your pet's food.

Cuttlebones that are approximately 10 in / 25.4 cm in length sell for around $3 / £1.87.

Note that vitamin D3 will likely only be available in a multivitamin formulation. These products in powdered form are available in a range of $10-$15 / £6-£9.

Leopard - Water and Humidity

The same kind of shallow "saucer" dish used with Sulcatas should be used with Leopard Tortoises. The tortoises will stand in the water while they drink, so get a dish large enough to accommodate their body size without tipping over.

Make sure that hatchlings are soaked in warm, shallow water, up to their necks, once or twice a week to stay well hydrated. Always change the water in the saucer and clean the receptacle after a soaking.

Fifteen minutes should be enough time for a good soak, but if your tortoise is drinking and seems to be enjoying himself, let it stay in the water as long as it likes.

Like Sulcatas, Leopard Tortoises should always have access to clean, fresh water. Adults should be soaked at least once a week.

Chapter 4 – Tortoise Health and Breeding

As in the previous chapter, the sub-headings in this chapter will be divided accordingly between "Sulcata" and "Leopard."

When you see a heading that is not preceded by a species name, the information in that section can be applied to both.

Tortoises and Heartwater

The infectious disease heartwater is commonly spread in Africa by ticks and affects cud-chewing animals or ruminants like cattle, sheep, and goats. The mortality rate from this disease is quite high, at 40-100%.

Chapter 4 – Tortoise Health and Breeding

In 1999, more than a dozen African bont ticks, carriers of heartwater, were discovered on imported Leopard and Sulcata Tortoises in the United States. Consequently, future importation of these creatures, and of Bell's Hingebacks was forbidden in 2000.

It is important to realize, however, that ticks not tortoises carry the heartwater disease. It is legal in the United States to move Leopard and Sulcata Tortoises across state lines, but the animals must have a health certificate from a qualified veterinarian stating they do not carry ticks.

When tortoises are purchased out of state in the U.S., it is standard practice for the buyer to pay an extra fee to obtain this health certification.

Specific Tortoise Health Conditions

Although both Sulcata and Leopard Tortoises have a reputation for being hardy and healthy animals, each is subject to some specific health conditions. Both species require a well-balanced diet and appropriate hydration to thrive.

Please note that the following is not a comprehensive health compendium, but simply an overview of the most common conditions seen in pet tortoises.

In the age of the Internet, tortoise owners have come to rely on each other in online discussion forums to find out more information about symptoms their pets are exhibiting.

It is highly recommended that you locate a qualified exotic animal veterinarian with experience treating tortoises before acquiring one as a pet.

To find a qualified veterinarian, please consult the homepage of the Association of Reptilian and Amphibian Veterinarians at ARAV.org, which includes international listings of members.

Pyramiding

Pyramiding of the shell in both Sulcata and Leopard Tortoises is primarily a consequence of a diet that contains too much protein, and of living conditions that are too low in humidity. Other contributing factors may include:

- Lack of calcium
- Over-abundance of phosphorous
- Inadequate levels of Vitamin D3 (from sunshine)
- Inadequate exercise
- Not enough fiber
- Not enough heat
- Poor hydration

Regardless of the specific cause, however, pyramiding is a form of metabolic bone disease in which the keratin on the scutes or scales of the shell builds up in a stacked fashion.

If the pyramiding is so severe that the shell becomes soft, the tortoise is in danger of suffering severe internal injuries.

Tortoises exhibiting pyramiding that are fed an appropriate grazing diet and allowed to roam in the sun for exercise will improve steadily. Their shells will harden over a period of months, and in some instance will even flatten out again.

Fungal and Bacterial Infections

If tortoises are kept in overly damp conditions, they are subject to both bacterial and fungal infections. Typical signs include:

- White patches on the skin
- Loose scutes on the shell
- Foul odor

Improvements in living conditions are key to correcting and preventing these infections, but it is best, if possible, to have the advice of a veterinarian before administering any type of medication.

Runny Nose Syndrome

Runny Nose Syndrome or RNS is not a disease per se, but an upper respiratory infection. Leopard Tortoises are more prone to developing RNS than Sulcatas.

RNS can develop at any age, and once a tortoise has RNS, it can be a carrier for life. A good quality diet and adequate exercise will go a long way toward ensuring that your pet does not develop RNS.

The use of antibiotic drops applied daily to the nasal chambers will be required to address this condition, which, if left untreated, can be life threatening.

Appropriate medications, available from a veterinarian, include, but are not limited to Oxytetracycline, Tylosin, and Baytril.

Pneumonia

Upper respiratory infections can also turn into pneumonia, but the condition is more likely caused by overly damp, cold conditions. Warning signs of pneumonia include:

- Stretching of the neck indicating difficulty breathing
- Breathing through the mouth
- Mucous evident in the nostrils and mouth
- Weakness in the legs
- Dehydration
- Depressed attitude

Tortoises with pneumonia also may run around blindly as a sign of the physical distress they are experiencing.

Pneumonia is a serious condition. Veterinarian intervention is required immediately. If any of these symptoms are evident in your tortoise, do not delay in contacting your vet and seeking treatment for your pet.

Other Health Problems

Other health problems that may be present in pet tortoises include, but are not limited to:

- Constipation from poor dietary management. Increase your pet's fiber intake, and soak the tortoise in tepid water for 30 minutes daily. Dandelion root may work as a mild laxative.

- Diarrhea from overfeeding. Add alfalfa to the diet temporarily, and remove any fruit products. If the feces are foul smelling or contain worms, contact a veterinarian.

- Vomiting. This is a serious sign in tortoises and is cause to immediately contact your veterinarian.

- Abscesses, especially near the ears, evident by an abnormal swelling. Abscesses can be caused by something as minor as the penetration of a thorn.

Abscessed lesions must be physically drained by a veterinarian and any dead tissue removed. Antibiotic treatment will also be required.

A range of internal and external parasites are also a potential threat in tortoises. Ticks can be removed manually by coating them with petroleum jelly to suffocate the insect and force it to release its jaws.

If signs of worms are present in your tortoise's feces, contact a veterinarian to obtain a proper deworming agent.

Remember that you are always the best preventive health care for your pet tortoise.

Observe your pet carefully on a daily basis. If you think something is wrong, it probably is. Never hesitate to seek the help of a qualified exotic animal veterinarian.

Sulcata - Breeding

In the wild, Sulcata Tortoises breed opportunistically year round. In captivity, they tend to follow the mating instinct most strongly in the fall when morning temperatures begin to drop.

Sulcata Courting Behavior

Males court the females in a fairly aggressive manner that involves both ramming and steering their prospective mates into obstacles in an effort to simply get them to stop.

In close quarters, overly enthusiastic males can cause severe shell damage to females. It's always a good idea to keep a close watch on the tortoises and to intervene if necessary.

Also, mating tortoises are surprisingly loud, so if you're living in close proximity to neighbors, you might want to warn them in advance!

Male Hormonal Aggression

Due to the excessive space requirements of the species, most people don't have room for more than a pair of Sulcatas, but one male will successfully breed with up to four females.

It's actually not a good idea to have multiple males unless you have plenty of room for the smaller, less aggressive ones to get away from the bigger dominant males.

If males are kept together, make sure you provide lots of hiding places, and have adequate shrubbery and physical features to simply disrupt the line of sight.

Often if males can't see one another, they will stop their pursuit and the fight is over. Do not, however, underestimate just how contentious male Sulcatas can be during mating season.

The principle tactic of an aggressive male is to flip the competition over on its back. This is much more dangerous than it might sound as a tortoise that is unable to right itself is highly susceptible to overheating and dying.

If you have multiple males in an enclosure, it's imperative to check for flipped tortoises several times a day during mating season. If the behavior becomes extreme, you may have to remove the smaller males from the enclosure temporarily.

Males will also bite, and fight with the gular spurs located on their throats. This can inflict serious damage to the head and neck of their opponent.

Since tortoises are prone to developing abscesses, check for wounds often during mating season, cleaning and treating any cuts and abrasions immediately before infection sets in.

Chapter 4 – Tortoise Health and Breeding

Female Nesting Behavior

Captive female Sulcatas will begin to nest 6-8 weeks after mating. The chosen site is usually at the base of a wall or other object in the pen or yard. The female digs a pit that slopes downward at the back end.

Once she is satisfied with the size and depth of the entrance, the female backs into the hole and begins to dig an egg chamber with her hind legs. This can take hours until she is completely satisfied with the space.

Do not be surprised to see normally docile female Sulcatas exhibit a high level of protective behavior toward their nests.

These confrontations typically involve ramming behavior that doesn't stop until the perceived threat -- including you -- has retreated to a safe distance.

The Sulcata Clutch

A female Sulcata can produce several clutches during a year, typically spacing them out by 30-40 days.

The average size of a clutch will be 12-24 eggs, although some individuals can lay as many as 40.

This prolific ability to reproduce explains, in part, the ready availability of Sulcata hatchlings, as evidenced by their prevalence at reptile shows.

Given the real and pressing problem of homeless and abandoned Sulcatas, please do not allow your tortoises to mate unless you have a plan for placing the hatchlings.

As soon as you are certain that the female has finished depositing her eggs, remove them from the nest and relocate them to an incubation box.

Incubating the Eggs

Place the collected eggs in a container and bury it halfway in a substrate of vermiculite. Keep the material moist, but not soaked. You are simply trying to create both warmth and humidity.

Use a thermometer, and make sure the eggs stay in a temperature range of 82-86 °F / 28-30 °C. The eggs should begin to hatch in 100 to 120 days.

Typically, the eggs will hatch over the course of a few days, but it can take as much as a month for the entire clutch to hatch. Beyond that point, any remaining eggs are not likely to be viable.

Hatchlings should be left in the incubator until they have mostly absorbed their egg yolks and then transferred to moistened paper towels until their plastrons have sealed.

Caring for Hatchlings

The most important thing to remember with hatchlings is to keep them warm and to preserve the humidity in their environment at around 80%. Use a combination thermometer and humidity gauge to monitor conditions.

The "cool" side of the habitat should be kept at 80-90 °F / 27-32 °C, with a basking spot on the other side at 100-110 °F / 38-43 °C. The babies will need 20-30 minutes of actual sunshine at least twice a week, but more is always better.

Maintain a 12-hour light/dark schedule with the hatchlings. They like it dark at night, but preserve the temperature in the habitat at night with a heating mat if necessary.

Since Sulcatas grow rapidly, expect to go through a series of progressively larger enclosures. You may well start out with a plastic storage bin and move toward a tortoise table according to the growth rate of the hatchlings.

Use a mulch or peat moss substrate, and keep it damp to help with the humidity levels. Provide at least one hide box, which should be at least partially buried in the substrate to provide privacy.

Feed the recommended Sulcata diet as laid out in the chapter on daily care, but obviously in smaller amounts commensurate with the size of the hatchlings. Always provide them with a saucer of water.

Remember, the tortoises should be able to walk into and out of the water, and the level should be no deeper than their necks.

Soak the hatchlings in shallow water at least once a day. Humidity becomes less critical when they reach 6-8 in / 15.24-20.32 cm in length.

Leopard - Breeding

Leopard Tortoises begin to breed in February and March in the Northern Hemisphere and continue into September at which time the females begin to nest.

Males actively search for females, walking or running into them while bobbing their heads to attract attention.

Females are equally agitated when selecting their nesting spots, pacing back and forth restlessly until they've made their choice.

Nesting

Females scrape the surface of the selected spot in circular motions using their long claws to loosen the dirt. Gradually, the female pushes the dirt to the sides, but the finished hole will be just large enough to accommodate the eggs.

If necessary, the female will use urine to moisten the dirt to a muddy consistency. The final cavity is roughly the shape of a flask, and will hold from 5-21 eggs. Female Leopard Tortoises nest 4-5 times per season.

When the nesting cavity is full, the female covers the hole and stamps the dirt down until it is difficult to tell that the area was ever disturbed.

At this point, you will want to carefully excavate the nest and remove the eggs to be transferred to an incubator.

Be extremely careful, as the eggs will be slippery from the mucous excreted during the laying process.

Incubation

Follow the same process for incubating the eggs as described above for Sulcata Tortoises. The appropriate temperature range for Leopard Tortoises is 82-86 °F / 28-30 °C with an incubation period of 88-163 days.

Caring for Hatchlings

The major difference in caring for Leopard Tortoise hatchlings is the appropriate temperature range to be established in the habitat.

The cool end should be kept in the mid-70s °F / 24 °C while the basking spot should be warmed to 95 °F / 35 °C.

Observe the same 12-hour light and dark cycle, turning the light off at night, but preserving the temperature in the habitat with a warming mat if necessary.

Follow the same guidelines for proper hydration as those suggested for Sulcata Tortoises, and increase the size of the habitat commensurate with the hatchlings' growth.

Afterword

In his article for Tortoise.org, "A Sulcata Here, A Sulcata There, A Sulcata Everywhere," David Friend concluded his excellent account of years spent with the giant creatures writing:

"Be considerate and responsible and continue to educate yourself on your animal's needs. With the proper care and environment you and your Sulcata will enjoy many years together. Be kind to Mother Nature; she keeps us in her care forever."

The purpose of this text has been to provide an overview of the care of the third and fourth largest land tortoises in the world, the Sulcata and the Leopard Tortoise.

Both have increased in popularity as pets over the last 20-30 years, to the point that far too many today are abandoned for the same reason that many people cite for being attracted to the creatures in the first place: their size.

Sulcatas get to be 2-3 ft (0.6-0.9 m) in length and tip the scales at 100-200 lbs (45.35-90.7 kg).

Leopard Tortoises measure 18-28 in (45.72-71.12 cm) and weigh between 40-120 lbs (18.14-54.43 kg).

These are not the kinds of tortoises that can be kept in aquariums. They grow fast, reaching or exceeding 100 lbs / 45.4 kg within five years.

Afterword

If, however, you can overcome the limitations of space, and can provide your tortoise with room to graze — and in the case of Sulcatas — dig, you will be rewarded with a genuinely affectionate companion.

Sulcatas and Leopard Tortoises are intelligent and good-natured, rarely showing aggression (which typically coincides with mating), but "running" to greet their keepers, and enjoying a nice shell rub in the sun.

It is essential to make sure — in advance — that you have access to an exotic animal veterinarian, and you must be able to provide heated shelter for your tortoise in the winter. Beyond that, however, keeping a tortoise is rather like keeping exotic "livestock."

Both species are grazing herbivores that like to wander about eating and checking things out. They get bored easily in small spaces.

Although both are indigenous to Africa, they must be provided with adequate shade and lots of clean water. Dehydration is a real and present danger with both species.

Sulcata and Leopard Tortoises are among the easiest of all exotic creatures to care for under the correct circumstances. They are not the right pet for everyone, but when all the pieces fall into place, these big tortoises are simply exceptional companions.

Relevant Websites

The EASIEST Way

Simply go to http://www.TortoiseBook.com and join free. We will provide you with 1 webpage with ALL these web addresses listed.

Amazon carry a fantastic range of tortoise products at very good prices. I highly recommend you take a look. You can buy food, heat mats, bedding and a LOT more

TortoiseBook.com/products.htm (USA)
TortoiseBook.com/productsuk.htm (UK)

Frankie Tortoise Tails

The Adventures of a 12-year-old Sulcata
http://www.frankietortoisetails.blogspot.com/

New York Turtle and Tortoise Society

http://www.nytts.org/

Turtle and Tortoise Forum

http://www.kingsnake.com

Chelonian Research Foundation

http://www.chelonian.org/

Reptile Channel

http://www.ReptileChannel.com

Sulcata Station

Relevant Websites

http://www.sulcata-station.org

The Sulcata and Leopard Tortoise
http://www.africantortoise.com/sulcata.htm

Ojai Sulcata Project
http://www.ojaisulcataproject.org

Great Site for Sulcata Tortoise Information
http://www.sulcatatortoise.net/

Tortoise Forum
http://www.tortoiseforum.org/

California Turtle and Tortoise Club
http://www.tortoise.org/archives/sulcata1.html

Tortoise Trust re: Leopard Tortoise
http://www.tortoisetrust.org/articles/leopards.htm

Care and Feeding of a Hatchling Leopard Tortoise
http://www.tortoiseyard.com/leopard_tortoise_hatchling_c are.htm

Smithsonian Zoological Park re: Leopard Tortoise
http://www.nationalzoo.si.edu/Animals/ReptilesAmphibia ns/Facts/FactSheets/Leopardtortoise.cfm

American Tortoise Rescue
http://www.tortoise.com

Mid-Atlantic Turtle and Tortoise Society

http://www.matts-turtles.org/adoptions.html

The World Chelonian Trust

http://www.chelonia.org/Articles/sulcatacare.htm

Rescue, Rehabilitation, Rehoming

http://www.turtopia.tripod.com

Association of Reptilian and Amphibians Veterinarians

http://www.arav.org

Melissa Kaplan's Herp Care Collection

http://www.anapsid.org

Don't forget

See all these resources in 1 place at
http://www.TortoiseBook.com

Tortoise - Frequently Asked Questions

Although we recommend that you read the entire text to fully understand the care requirements of Sulcata and Leopard Tortoises, the following are some of the most frequently asked questions about tortoises in general.

If my tortoise needs a calcium supplement, can I just grind up eggshells and mix them in with my pet's food?

The use of eggshells as a source of calcium is not a good idea for a number of reasons.

First, they don't really have that much calcium content! Second, you are running a high risk of infecting your tortoise with salmonella.

Instead, simply obtain calcium carbonate in bulk from any feed store or use a human calcium supplement. These products are inexpensive, and far safer than using eggshells.

If tortoises are not meat eaters, how do they get protein in their diets? Don't they need at least some meat to stay healthy?

This is the same argument that human vegetarians must answer on an almost daily basis!

There are perfectly good levels of protein in the plant material — including seeds and grasses — that are the preferred diet for tortoises.

The digestive tracts of these animals are specially adapted to this kind of diet. Many big mammals (like elephants) are herbivores and they are obviously thriving on a plant-only diet.

In fact, some plant material has too much protein to be safely used with tortoises, including:

- Alfalfa
- Bean sprouts
- Beans

- Peas

An overabundance of protein in a tortoise's diet can lead to severe kidney problems and even renal failure.

Since tofu is made from vegetable sources, can I use that to make sure my tortoise is getting enough protein?

A healthy tortoise that is receiving the correct plant-based diet for its digestive system does not need any "extras."

Substances like tofu simply have too much protein, which is dangerous for tortoises, putting them at high risk for kidney problems and renal failure.

The idea that your tortoise needs more protein than it receives from its natural diet will, in the long run, only hurt your pet.

I bought my tortoise at a pet store and was told I just needed to give it lettuce and fruit. Is that right?

Understand that pet stores are interested in making sales. It is highly unlikely that the person with whom you were dealing has more than a cursory understanding of the real dietary and environmental needs of the tortoise you purchased.

All tortoises have highly specific diets that must be followed in order to provide the animal with the nutrition it needs as well as to avoid substances — like lettuce — that could do serious harm to the animal's system.

Never go on the advice of a clerk in a pet store, no matter how well meaning that advice may be. Research the animal in which you are interested in advance of a purchase and understand its specific needs fully.

In the case of Sulcata Tortoises, a diet of lettuce would cause the tortoise to become quite ill, while a Leopard Tortoise would be more tolerant.

Neither species, however, should be given any significant amount of fruit.

Can my tortoise eat things like hard-boiled eggs and cheese?

Think about your question. There is no source in the wild for a tortoise to have access to either cheese or hard-boiled eggs. Such items, along with a host of other "goodies" are not natural foods and are in no way good for your tortoise.

It is an unfortunate tendency of many pet owners to try to share "human" food with their pets. Just because the animal eats the item doesn't mean the food is good for it.

There's a white substance in my tortoise's urine that looks like chalk. Is it getting more calcium than it should?

What you are seeing is probably uric acid, not calcium. In reptiles and birds, uric acid is a natural by-product of the metabolism of protein.

Seeing some of this material in the urine is normal, but if it seems to be present in excess, it's possible your pet is not eating a well-balanced diet.

Can I regulate the amount of calcium my tortoise receives through diet alone?

For the most part, yes, if you ensure that your pet eats a well-balanced diet including hay raised on soil with a good calcium level. This information is often, however, quite difficult to acquire.

Making sure that your tortoise has enough calcium is really just as simple as buying it a big cuttlebone to chew on, or crushing up calcium tablets and adding the powder to your pet's food a couple of times a week.

Instead of thinking in terms of "one" thing creating good health for your tortoise, look at all the factors that go into tortoise husbandry. In combination, these things ensure good balance for your pet.

Why do some sources recommend that the calcium supplement used with a pet tortoise be free of phosphorus?

While phosphorus is also an important element of your pet's diet, the tortoise should get all the phosphorus it requires from the green plants and vegetables it consumes.

Herbivores like tortoises are much more likely to be deficient in calcium, and this is the supplementation for which you should strive.

It is highly unlikely that your pet will lack for phosphorous if you are feeding the tortoise the appropriate plant material.

So is it okay to use calcium carbonate as a supplement?

Calcium carbonate is perfectly safe as long as your tortoise is getting adequate levels of Vitamin D3 from time in the sun, and if the diet has safe levels of plant protein.
It is possible that your tortoise will need additional mineral supplementation, but this is dependent on the quality of produce you are able to acquire.

Typically organic produce and hay grown in high quality soil will give your tortoise all the mineral content it needs.

If mineral supplements are used, the products can be obtained at a reptile supply house and should be given once or twice a week.

My tortoise spends a lot of time outside. Do I need to worry about giving it oral Vitamin D3?

Tortoises that are fortunate enough to be able to spend their days outside will be getting all the Vitamin D3 they require without a need for oral supplements.

If, however, you live in regions that get a lot of cloud cover, your pet may need supplementation.

It's best to try to find other, more experienced tortoise owners in your region for guidance on the supplementation regimen they follow.

Do tortoises need a Vitamin A supplement?

On a well-balanced and species appropriate diet, a tortoise will not require Vitamin A supplementation.

What about using liquid sunshine D3 drops? They're a lot cheaper than UVB lighting.

The use of such products is very dangerous as you can easily overdose your pet.

There is no substitute for real sunshine in the life of your tortoise, and for the times when it must be indoors for extended periods, UVB lighting is an essential habitat component.

Is obesity a problem with pet tortoises?

Absolutely. Unfortunately, obesity is a problem with all companion species, and tortoises are not immune to this health problem.

Sulcata Tortoises have something of a reputation for weight problems because they like to eat things they shouldn't.

Allowing your tortoise to become overweight creates serious long-term health worries, including the development of a fatty liver.

Always remember that Leopard and Sulcata Tortoises are grazing herbivores and should not be fed a high-fat or high-protein diet.

Sulcata Frequently Asked Questions

Sulcata Tortoises husbandry is a fairly complicated business. It's best to read the entire text to really know how to care for your pet and to understand what is needed to create an optimal environment.

These are some of the most frequently asked questions about this species, but the better you get to know your tortoise, the more information you'll want at your disposal.

It cannot be emphasized enough that getting a pet as large and as long lived as a Sulcata Tortoise should never be undertaken lightly or as an impulse buy.

Learn everything you can about these creatures long before you bring one home. Also make sure – in advance – that you will be able to access the services of a qualified exotic pet veterinarian, preferably one with experience treating tortoises.

How long does a Sulcata Tortoise live?

With proper care, a Sulcata Tortoise can live for 50-150 years in captivity.

How big will a Sulcata Tortoise grow to be?

Adults of the species are 2 – 3 feet (60 – 90cm) long and weigh an impressive 100-200 lbs (45 - 90 kg).

How much room does a Sulcata Tortoise need?

Hatchlings can live on a tortoise table, but your Sulcata will grow rapidly, attaining a size of 100 lbs / 45.45 kg in less than 5 years.

The generally accepted estimates for grazing and roaming space are one half to one acre per tortoise.

What should I feed my Sulcata Tortoise?

A Sulcata Tortoise should not be fed a diet that consists mainly of produce from the grocery store. These products are too rich for the animal's system. The regular diet should consist of grasses, weeds, and clovers.

Given their region of origin south of the Sahara Desert, Sulcatas do best on high fiber foods with relatively low nutrients.

Feeding these creatures overly rich foods can cause kidney and liver damage, shortening the lifespan of the tortoise.

Additionally, feeding nothing but a diet of vegetables will make your tortoise grow too rapidly, leading to shell distortions and weakened bone structure.

Can I feed my Sulcata fruit?

Sulcatas love fruit, but don't give it to them! These tortoises have beneficial bacteria in their intestines that are integral to their digestive process. The acids and sugars in fruit changes the acidity of the digestive tract and can kill off these vital bacteria.

If this occurs, and toxins move out of the gut and into the bloodstream, the tortoise can experience a form of toxic shock syndrome.

Why do I need to soak my Sulcata Tortoise?

In the wild, Sulcatas create high humid microclimates in their burrows. Tortoises that live in captivity don't have access to this unique form of hydration.

As an added problem, some individuals will not drink voluntarily. Soaking the tortoise regularly prevents potentially deadly dehydration.

Soak hatchlings in lukewarm water up to their necks for 15 minutes a day. At one year of age, switch to three soakings per week.

As the tortoise increases in size, you can gradually cut back to once a week. Use plastic tubs, and increase the sizes as the tortoise grows.

Even if you think your tortoise is not drinking, provide clean water at all times. Use the large saucers that go under flowerpots so the tortoises can walk right in. They will either drink, or flip on their backs and soak on their own.

These saucers will tend to develop algae growth. Use vinegar only to clean away the algae and let the saucer dry in the sunlight away from the tortoise. Keep several of these dishes on hand to rotate them out as necessary.

There's a bubbling discharge coming out of my tortoise's nose. Why?

Discharge from the nose indicates illness. You need to get your pet to the veterinarian. Tortoises are at risk for developing the equivalent of a bad cold or even pneumonia called Runny Nose Syndrome (RNS).

If not treated with antibiotics, the infection can be fatal. Tortoises kept in damp, cool climates are at a higher risk of developing RNS.

The use of antibiotics can stress the tortoise's kidneys. The animal must be kept warm and well hydrated to counteract this side effect and to assist its immune system in fighting off the infection.

My tortoise is walking back and forth and trying to climb the corners of its pen. Why?

The behavior you describe is an expression of boredom. If your tortoise is small enough to still be living on a tortoise table, make the walls opaque so your pet can't see through them.

Create a more stimulating environment for the tortoise by adding boxes and plants, and more or less building an "obstacle course." Block the corners off and encourage the tortoise to explore within the confines of its table or other enclosure.

Note that this kind of behavior can even be exhibited if the tortoise has the run of your whole backyard. Be prepared to mix things up for your pet by moving things around and creating new hiding and climbing places.

Sulcatas are natural born, roaming explorers. To keep them happy, you have to constantly supply them with new adventures.

Leopard Tortoise Frequently Asked Questions

Keeping a Leopard Tortoise is an involved process, and it is recommended that you read the entire text for a full understanding of how to care for your pet.

The following, however, are some of the most frequently asked questions about this species.

Do not acquire a Leopard Tortoise as an impulse buy. These creatures are large and live a long time.

Know exactly what you're getting into before you bring one home!

Leopard Tortoise Frequently Asked Questions

How big does a Leopard Tortoise get?

An adult Leopard Tortoise will measure 18-28 inches (45.72-71.12 cm) in length and will weigh between 40-120 lbs (18.14-54.43 kg).

How long will a Leopard Tortoise live?

A well cared for Leopard Tortoise should live 80 to 100 years in captivity.

Why are they called "Leopard" Tortoises?

The shell of this species is covered with black spots that sometimes look like dashes or even stripes. Every shell is different, and set against the light yellow or cream-colored background, the effect looks like the coat of a leopard.

How much will a Leopard Tortoise cost?

Price depends entirely on where you buy, and on the size of the tortoise at purchase.

Hatchlings are typically sold in a range of $90-$150 / £56.20-£93.70, while adults are priced anywhere up to $1000 / £625 each.

Do Leopard Tortoises have a good disposition?

Yes. Leopard Tortoises are actually rather shy, and enjoy having places to hide. They rarely show aggression, and males can be housed together without fighting.

As pets, Leopard Tortoises will respond well to their owners, and enjoy interaction and affection.

How can I tell if a Leopard Tortoise is healthy?

The tortoise should be active and alert, eating and drinking well, and have expressive, interested eyes. Some owners go so far as to say tortoises have a "twinkle" in their eyes.

The animal's nostrils should be clear of any discharge, and there should be no signs of dehydration. The shell should not feel soft, and there should be no foul odor from the shell or skin.

What kind of diet does my Leopard Tortoise need?

Leopard Tortoises require a diet that is rich in calcium and high in fiber in keeping with their natural lifestyle as grazing herbivores.

They should be fed a diet of hay, supplemented with vegetables, and a very low amount of fruit.

(See the chapter in this book on daily care for more detailed dietary instructions.)

What kind of water dish should I use?

Pick a saucer instead of a bowl. Your Leopard Tortoise needs to be able to stand in the water while it's drinking.

The saucer should be big enough that the tortoise can't tip it over, and the water should not be any deeper than your pet's neck.

Is it a good idea to breed Leopard Tortoises?

There is a decided problem with Sulcata and Leopard Tortoises being abandoned. Rescue groups are overwhelmed with tortoises that need new homes.

It is not a good idea to add to this over-population problem, and given the space requirements of these large tortoises, you may have difficulty finding room for one, much less several.
In general, breeding by enthusiasts is a practice I discourage.

Can I buy my Leopard Tortoise online?

You can buy Leopard Tortoises online, but again, this is not a practice I encourage. No matter what guarantees may be offered by the retailer, shipping a live animal is simply cruel.

Additionally, these creatures can be fatally harmed by shell damage in transit, and dehydration is a very real concern. Buying online is not a good idea.

Glossary

A

Anal - This term may either refer to the region around the end of an animal's digestive tract, or to a suture on the tortoise's plastron.

Anterior - A spatial term referring to the front portion of an animal where the head is located.

Antibiotic - Antibiotics are medications developed synthetically in laboratory settings from fungi and other microorganisms that are used to kill harmful bacteria in living organisms.

Arid - Any geographic region that gets less than 9.8 in / 25 cm of rain per year is classified as being an "arid" climate.

Arid habitat - Arid habitats are designed for animals like African tortoises to create an environment similar to that of their native regions with rocky or sandy soil and low humidity levels.

B

Bask - Basking is a behavior in many animals, but especially in reptiles, that involves lying in warm, sunny areas or under heat lamps to absorb the warmth into their bodies.

Glossary

Basking light - A basking light may be either an actual bulb, or a heating element, that is provided in a reptile enclosure to create an area of warmth for the animal to enjoy.

Basking spot - The basking spot is the area directly under a heated light or element that a reptile uses to bask and absorb heat into its body. This spot is always hotter than the temperature in the surrounding habitat.

Baytril - Baytril is a medication often used to treat Runny Nose Syndrome in tortoises. It is the trade name used for the medication enrofloxacin, which is an antibacterial agent.

Body temperature - Body temperature is a measure of the interior temperature of the body rather than an exterior reading. It is normally taken in tortoises with a thermometer inserted in the cloaca.

Breed - In any species, the breed refers to a set of characteristics that are consistently identifiable and that are passed from parents to offspring that distinguish a specific strain from other equally unique types found within the same species.

Brumation - This state should not be confused with hibernation, but is rather a time during cool weather when tortoises tend to sleep most of the time and do not eat much. In this regard, brumation may be referred to as "semi-hibernation."

Buccal - A term referring to anything in relation to the mouth.

Burrow - Burrowing is a behavior in which animals create underground shelters for themselves. These shelters may serve as places to hide and/or sleep and as a place to conceal food stores. Sulcata tortoises create elaborate burrows connected by tunnels that serve as humid microclimates.

C

Calcium - Calcium is a mineral necessary for bone development and health. In captivity, if tortoises do not receive adequate dietary calcium, it may be necessary to supplement their diet with cuttlebones or powdered calcium added to their food. Calcium and phosphorous work together in the formation of healthy bone tissue, but typically tortoises derive adequate amounts of phosphorous from their food alone. A deficiency of calcium can contribute to the development of metabolic bone disease.

Captive bred - Any animal that was not captured in the wild, but was rather born or hatched in captivity and is the product of parents who mated in captivity is said to be captive bred.

Captive hatched - Similar to the term captive bred, the phrase captive hatch refers to animals hatched from eggs while kept by humans.

Glossary

Carapace - The outer shell that covers the body of a tortoise or turtle is properly called the carapace.

Caudal or caudally - Terms referring to the tail of a creature or indicating a bodily feature on the body in the area of the tail.

Chelonian - A group of reptiles including turtles, tortoises, and terrapins that are characterized by their shell coverings.

Clutch - The entire number or set of eggs that are deposited or laid at the same time by one individual parent.

Cold-blooded - When the metabolism and body temperature of an animal are reliant on external temperature for regulation, the creature is said to be cold-blooded. Another term for this state is ectothermic.

Cranial - The proper term for references to an animal's skull.

Cutaneous - A reference to the surface layer of an animal's skin.

Cuttlebone - A cuttlebone is actually the shell of the cuttlefish. It is white, and has the texture of pumice. Cuttlebones are typically used with pet birds and reptiles as a source of calcium supplementation.

Glossary

D

Dehydration - When a creature does not get enough water in its system due to an overly hot and arid environment or a lack of supplied water, dehydration is the serious depletion of water in the tissues of the body that can, if left unaddressed, lead to shock and death.

Dorsal - The proper anatomical term for references to an animal's back or the upper part of its body.

E

Ears - Tortoises do not have true ears, but rather tympanic membranes. These sensitive structures are one of the most common sites where abscesses may form on these animals.

Ectothermic - The proper term for animals that are said to be "cold blooded." These creatures rely on the ambient temperature in their environment for the regulation of their own body temperature and for the correct functioning of their metabolisms.

Endothermic - The proper term for animals that are capable of generating their own body warmth and thus regulating their own metabolism.

G

Gestation - Gestation is the elapsed time between fertilization of an egg and the time when that egg is actually expelled or laid from the body of the female.

Gular - The gular scutes in tortoises are located behind and directly below the head.

Gut - The digestive or alimentary canal, beginning in the mouth and extending through the intestine to the cloaca may be referred to collectively as the "gut."

Gut flora -Beneficial microflora and protozoa that live in the digestive tract of animals and humans and aid in proper digestion are called gut flora.

H

Habitat - Any environment, natural or artificially engineered, in which an animal lives on a daily basis.

Hatchling - In animals that emerge from eggs at birth, the term "hatchling" refers to the creatures during their first 6 months of life.

Herbivore - Animals that live exclusively on a diet of plant material and / or grasses.

Hibernation - During cold weather some animals enter a state in which their body temperature, blood pressure, rate of respiration, and metabolic rate drop into a kind of suspended animation or dormancy called hibernation. During this period, the animal uses body fat reserves to survive, awakening when the weather starts to get warmer.

Glossary

I

Incubation - Incubation is the artificial process by which eggs are taken from a parent and hatched via a program of human husbandry.

Incubation period - The elapsed period of time from the point at which an egg has been laid until the embryo has developed to the point of emerging.

J

Juvenile - Young creatures at the stage of their development before sexual maturity is attained.

K

Keratin - Keratin is the main component making up the carapace or shell, as well as the beak and claws of tortoises. It is a hard protein composed of strands of tough fiber.

L

Lateral - A spatial term referring to the sides of a creature.

M

Metabolic bone disease (MBD) - This disease, which is common to tortoises, is a consequence of dietary imbalances or deficiencies. It can manifest as pyramiding,

Glossary

an overall softening of the shell, or in hatchlings as the malformation of bones.

O

Opportunistic - A term referring to the tendency of an animal to do something in response to a chance or situation that simply presents itself, like eating a particular substance, or mating when a member of the opposite gender is encountered rather than at a set time of year.

P

Parasite - Organisms that live in or on other creatures and cannot exist independent of those creatures for means of shelter and nourishment are said to be parasitic in nature.

Pathogen - An agent that causes a disease is said to be a pathogen, for example a virus or a bacterium.

Plastron - In turtles and tortoises, the underside of the shell is referred to as the plastron.

Poikilotherm - Another term for animals whose body temperature changes in accord with the temperature of their surrounding environment.

R

Range - Range is the area, in terms of geography, over which a species is found in nature.

Glossary

Reptile - Reptiles are cold-blooded vertebrates that lay eggs. Examples include turtles, tortoises, snakes, lizards, and crocodiles. Most are covered by scales or plates and breathe via lungs.

Runny nose syndrome (RNS) - This condition, seen often in tortoises, may be caused by a fungus, bacterium, or virus. All manifest as an upper respiratory infection, and have the potential to develop into pneumonia. RNS requires immediate treatment by an exotic animal veterinarian.

S

Salmonella - The disease salmonella, which can be transmitted to humans by animals and is particularly associated with pet reptiles, is caused by a strain of gram negative bacteria. In humans, it manifests as severe gastrointestinal distress much like food poisoning.

Savannah - Areas of grassy, open plains and low vegetation are described as savannahs.

Scutes - On the shells of turtles and tortoises, the individual plates, which appear as distinct sections, are properly termed "scutes." They are composed of keratin.

Supplements - In captivity, in order to maintain the correct dietary balance, it may be necessary to add or supplement vitamins and minerals, typically via a powder or liquid concentrated addition to their food.

Glossary

Sutures - On the shell of a turtle or tortoise, the individual spaces or seams between the plates or scutes are called sutures.

T

Terrestrial - Creatures that spend the majority of their lives on land.

Tortoise - Members of the order testudinidae that are essentially terrestrial turtles. They tend to have rounded, high shells and club-like, thick limbs.

Turtle - Members of the order testudinidae that are semi-terrestrial or marine dwellers. Often the terms turtle and tortoise are used interchangeably.

V

Vertebral - A term referring to the region of the spine that is also used to designate the row of scutes on the shell of a tortoise that run centrally at the top of the carapace.

Vertebrate - Animals, including reptiles, whose skeletons are internal.

Vent - The area under or at the base of the tail where waste and eggs exit the body.

Ventral - A spatial term referring to the underside of an animal. The direct opposite of the term dorsal.

Glossary

W

Wild caught - Any animal that has been captured in its native setting and transferred to life in captivity.

Y

Yolk - The interior portion of a developing egg that provides nutrients to the growing fetus.

Yolk sac - Hatchling tortoises emerge from the egg with the remnants of the egg yolks attached to their plastrons encased in a yolk sac from which they will continue to draw nutrition for the first days of their lives.

Z

Zoonosis - Any infectious disease that can be transmitted to humans from animals.

Index

abandoned, 18, 23, 36, 38, 39

abnormal swelling, 69

Abscesses, 69

active, 18, 23, 35

Aldabra Tortoise, 11

alfalfa, 53, 69

apartment dwellers, 28

aquarium, 23, 37

Baytril, 68

brassicae family, 52

breeding, 16

burrows, 15, 18, 94

calcium, 52, 54, 55, 59, 60, 62, 66

calcium-phosphorous balance, 52

cat, 24

children, 25

clutches, 20, 73

color, 20

concave plastron, 17

Constipation, 69

cuttlebone, 55

Dandelion root, 69

deworming agent, 70

Diarrhea, 69

diet, 16, 41, 51, 52, 53, 55, 60, 61, 62, 65, 66, 67, 69, 76, 93, 94

dietary needs, 11

diseases, 38

dish, 47

dog, 24, 25

edible flowers, 53

eggs, 16, 20

enclosures, 59, 75

exotic species, 38

eyes, 26, 35

Females, 17

fiber, 48, 50, 94

fiber intake, 69

food, 16

fungal infections, 67

Galapagos Tortoise, 11

Geochelone gigantea, 11

Geochelone nigra, 11

grasses, 13, 16, 52, 54, 93

grazing diet, 67

Greek Tortoise, 15

growth rate, 76

gular spurs, 72

Hatchlings, 57, 93

head, 26, 35

health, 34

Index

Suggestions / Reviews

I really hope you liked the book and found it useful.

A LOT of time and hard work went into writing it. I have loved these tortoises for years and thought it was about time I put some knowledge down on paper for others to use.

Almost certainly you purchased this book online so I'm sure you'll be contacted soon asking for your review of it by the book seller you ordered it through. I would be very, very grateful if you could provide a positive review please.

However if you are unhappy with the book or feel I have missed information out then please do get in contact first (before leaving the review) and hopefully I can help.

I'm happy to rewrite / add sections if you feel it would improve the book for other readers in the future. Simply email me

william@tortoisebook.com

with your suggestions and I'll get back to you as soon as I can (it may take a few days) If I can I will then act on your ideas and revise the book and send you a free copy (and others who joined our free club via http://www.tortoisebook.com) with the updated book ASAP just as a 'thank you' for helping to improve it.

Thank you again

William Clinton